BLACK HOLES

ENERGY

GALAXIES

GRAVITY

LIGHT

MYSTERIES OF THE UNIVERSE

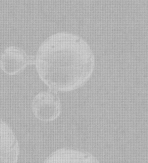

MASS & MATTER

SPACE & TIME

STARS

MYSTERIES OF THE UNIVERSE

Black Holes

JIM WHITING

CREATIVE EDUCATION

Published by Creative Education

P.O. Box 227, Mankato, Minnesota 56002

Creative Education is an imprint of The Creative Company

www.thecreativecompany.us

Design and production by Blue Design

Art direction by Rita Marshall

Printed in the United States of America

Photographs by Corbis (Bettmann, Dusko Despotovic, NASA/JPL-Caltech, Reuters, MARTIAL TREZZINI, Underwood & Underwood), Getty Images (Paul E. Alers/NASA, MARK GARLICK, MARK GARLICK/SPL, Hulton Archive, MAGRATH PHOTOGRAPHY/NIELSEN, Paul Popper/Popperfoto, Popperfoto, Antonio M. Rosario, Stocktrek, Stocktrek Images, Visuals Unlimited, Inc./Victor Habbick), iStockphoto (arne thaysen), NASA (J. J. Hester [Arizona State University], NASA/CXC/ASU/J. Hester et al., NASA/ ESA/SSC/CXC/STScI, H. Richer [University of British Columbia])

Cover and folio illustration © 2011 Alex Ryan

Library of Congress Cataloging-in-Publication Data

Whiting, Jim

Black holes / by Jim Whiting.

p. cm. — (Mysteries of the universe)

Includes bibliographical references and index.

Summary: An examination of the science behind the astronomical phenomena known as black holes, including relevant theories and history-making discoveries as well as topics of current and future research.

ISBN 978-1-60818-186-5

1. Black holes (Astronomy)—Juvenile literature. I. Title.

QB843.B55W45 2012

523.8'875—dc23   2011040137

First Edition

9 8 7 6 5 4 3 2 1

American physicist Albert Michelson

TABLE OF CONTENTS

Our solar system revolves around the sun

INTRODUCTION

For most of human history, the true nature of the universe was shrouded in myth and mystery. About 400 years ago, scientists began unraveling those mysteries. Their efforts were so successful that American **physicist** Albert Michelson wrote in 1894, "The more important fundamental laws and facts of physical science have all been discovered, and these are now so firmly established that the possibility of their ever being supplemented in consequence of new discoveries is exceedingly remote." William Thomson, Baron Kelvin, perhaps that era's most famous physicist, echoed Michelson: "There is nothing new to be discovered in physics now. All that remains is more and more precise measurement." Both men were wrong. Within a few years, scientists had revealed the makeup of the tiny **atom** and the unexpected vastness of outer space. Yet the universe doesn't yield its mysteries easily, and much remains to be discovered.

Black holes are the "new kids on the block" in this hall of scientific mysteries, as scientists began studying them only a few decades ago. They present a unique problem—they can't be observed. To see anything, we need light. But the pull of gravity inside black holes is so strong that nothing, not even light, can escape. As a result, scientists have to use special tools to investigate black holes. Even today, people can't say with absolute certainty that black holes exist. However, they remain some of the most tantalizing and fascinating of all the universe's mysteries.

Irish-born physicist Baron Kelvin

INTRODUCTION

9

APPETITE FOR GRAVITY

Gigantic, cosmic Godzillas, grabbing up everything around them and gulping it all down into an impossibly deep pit from which there is no escape. This is the prevailing public image of black holes, which noted British physicist Stephen Hawking terms the "bad boys of the universe." As American science writer Isaac Asimov has pointed out, "Since 1960 the universe has taken on a whole new face.... and the most exciting, most mysterious, most violent, and most extreme phenomena of all has the simplest, plainest, calmest, and mildest name—nothing more than a black hole."

No one has ever seen a black hole, and there's a good reason why. Even though light is the fastest thing in the universe, traveling at a rate of 186,282 miles (299,792 km) per second, it cannot pierce the darkness of a black hole. What could possibly slow light down, or even more improbably, stop it altogether?

The answer is gravity, one of the most fundamental forces in the universe. Gravity not only keeps us firmly grounded on Earth rather than flying off into space, but it also keeps the planets in **orbit** around the sun. In its most basic form, gravity is the attraction between two masses. Every object, from a tiny atom to a star millions of times larger than Earth, has mass. Mass is the amount of matter a particular object contains.

The mass of an object—no matter how large or small it may be—attracts other objects toward it. Unless an object, such as a planet or a moon, has an exceedingly large amount of mass, gravity can't be felt. Mass isn't the same as weight. Weight measures the pull of gravity between two objects. On Earth, a person might weigh 150 pounds (68 kg). On the moon, that person's weight would drop to about 25 pounds (11.3 kg) because the moon has less mass than Earth. In space, a person's weight would drop to almost zero because there is no gravity pulling the body downward. Yet the mass of the person would remain the same in all three environments.

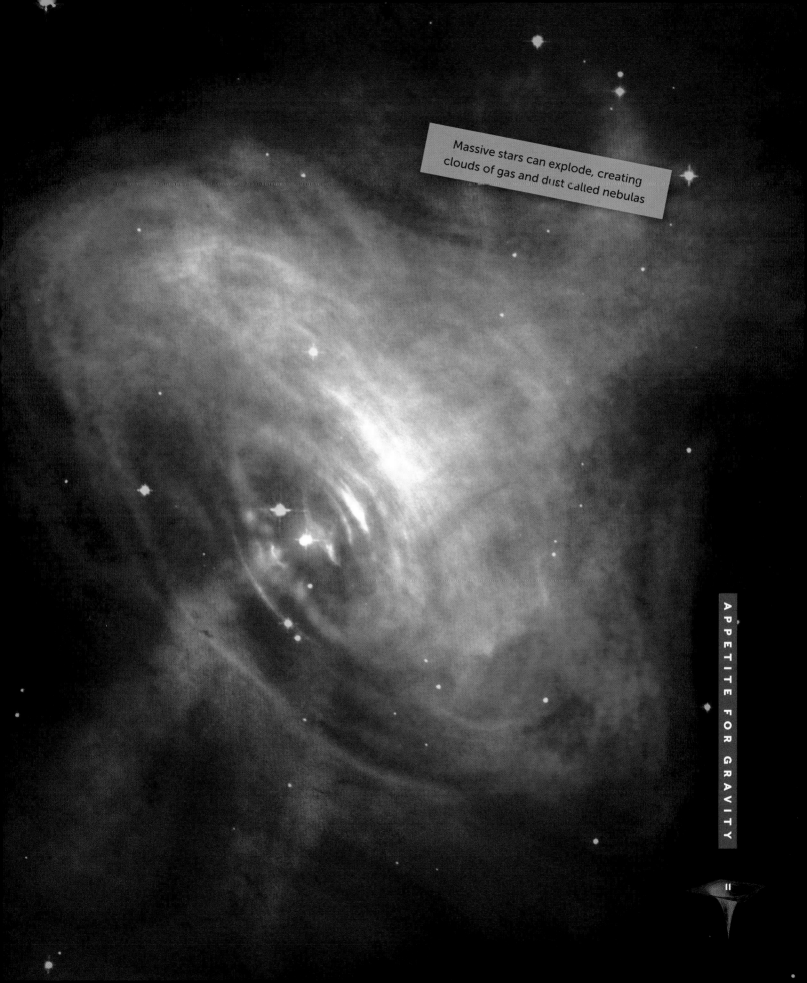

Massive stars can explode, creating clouds of gas and dust called nebulas

Rockets have to attain escape velocity to reach space

A black hole represents gravity's ultimate triumph over mass and matter. To understand how this happens, we must first grasp the concept of escape velocity. This is the speed at which something must travel in order to escape the pull of gravity. On Earth, escape velocity is 7 miles (11.3 km) per second, or 25,200 miles (40,555 km) per hour. At that speed, you could travel completely around the world in just one hour.

f you throw a ball into the air, it will rise a few feet and then come back. No one could ever throw a ball fast enough or high enough to approach escape velocity on Earth. It would be a different story on the Martian moons of Deimos and Phobos, though. Each is just a few miles in diameter and has such weak gravity that you could literally play catch with yourself. Just toss the ball in one direction, then turn around. Soon the ball would come back to you after completing an orbit. On our much larger Earth, not even jet airplanes can come close to escape velocity. Only massive rockets can rise fast enough to escape the pull of gravity and hurtle themselves into space. With black holes, though, escape velocity is simply impossible.

What causes black holes to form and gives them this almost inconceivable gravity? Scientists believe that they come from stars. A star is a gaseous collection of hydrogen and helium that burns at incredibly hot temperatures, often for billions of years. While the star is active, the force of gravity pushing inward on the star is balanced by the pressure of the burning gas as it expands outward. This principle is similar to what happens when you push on a balloon—the inflated air pushes back.

When a star begins to collapse, the hydrogen it burns begins to decline in the same manner as air leaking out of a balloon. The star can no longer resist gravity with as much force as it used to. At its peak, the star might have been millions of miles in diameter. Now the remaining material becomes packed into an area just a few miles wide. The gravity of the mass becomes continuously stronger until nothing can escape its pull. It becomes a black hole.

Another theory is that black holes are created when giant stars explode. If a star with more than three times the mass of the sun explodes to form a **supernova**, the force of the explosion can hurl a huge cloud of matter deep into space. At that point, gravity takes over and compresses what remains of the exploded star into an incredibly dense mass, forming a black hole.

A black hole is so powerful that it even bends space around itself. If you were to put a bowling ball in the middle of a blanket, and you held on to two corners, while a friend held on to the other two, the flat blanket would bend around the heavy mass in its center. Black holes' mass cause them to function in much the same way.

Astronomers believe that a black hole looks like a funnel with a flap on top and a long, thin tube at the bottom. Partway down the inside of the funnel is what is called the event horizon. Anything outside the event horizon is safe. As soon as something crosses the edge, though, it gets sucked farther down into the tube. It goes all the way to the bottom, which is called the singularity—a point at which matter becomes infinitely dense, and space and time become **infinitesimal**. Once an object arrives at the singularity, it can never escape. To escape, it would have to travel faster than the speed of light, and nothing can travel that fast. So light itself is swallowed up.

If you could somehow be transported across trillions of miles of space to a black hole, what would happen? Theoretically, you could get close to the event horizon without being in danger. You could even orbit it. But if you were not careful, you could get sucked in. For a brief period, you wouldn't feel anything because you would be in free fall. Then gravity would take over, and your feet would accelerate more rapidly

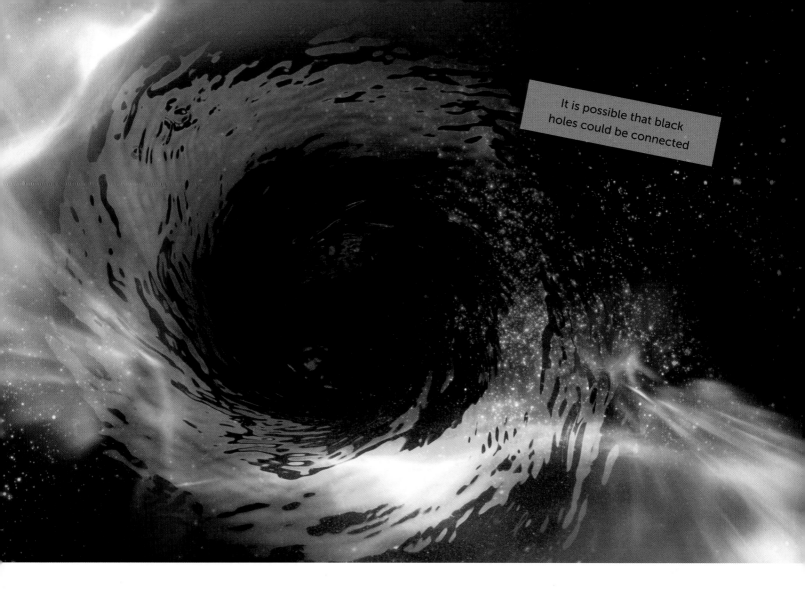

It is possible that black holes could be connected

than your head. Your body would begin to stretch. Soon you would become much taller and resemble a piece of slender pasta, which is why this process is referred to as "spaghettification." Your body wouldn't be able to withstand such violent changes, and it would snap in two, probably around your stomach.

That would set off a chain reaction in which your two halves would quickly snap in half again. Those four parts would become eight and so on until the disintegration reached the molecular and atomic levels. "And then, of course, the atoms themselves snap apart, leaving an unrecognizable parade of particles that, minutes earlier, had been you," concludes American **astrophysicist** Neil deGrasse Tyson. Despite the prospect of this theoretically dismal fate, black holes represent something beautiful to many scientists, as they may provide essential information about the very formation of the universe.

German-born physicist Albert Einstein

MAKING UP FOR LOST TIME

Unlike other heavenly bodies such as the moon, sun, planets, and stars—which have been observed and studied for thousands of years—black holes are a recent development in astronomical history. The first faint hint of their existence came just over two centuries ago, but that hint was not pursued. It wasn't until German physicist Albert Einstein announced his general theory of relativity in 1915 that the concept re-emerged. Another half century passed before the term "black holes" was coined by American physicist John Wheeler. The obvious explanation for the delayed discovery is that black holes are not easily detectable, even by the most powerful optical telescopes that were available to astronomers from the 1600s on. It wasn't until the 1960s advent of more sophisticated instruments using other wavelengths on the **electromagnetic spectrum**—from **radio waves** to **gamma rays**—that black holes began revealing their secrets.

Progress in unlocking these secrets had been delayed because many prominent scientists and astronomers, including Einstein, believed that stars eventually burned out and became little more than dead rocks floating in space. British astrophysicist Sir Arthur Eddington dismissed any other possibility as "stellar **buffoonery**." Despite the doubters, research into the life and death of stars continued. All stars have one feature in common. They produce heat and light through **nuclear fusion** reactions in their cores. These reactions continue unceasingly for millions or even billions of years. The energy these reactions produce balances the inward push of gravity on a star. Eventually, the hydrogen of which stars are composed begins to give out, and one of three things happens, depending on the size of the star.

In stars similar to our sun, gravity squeezes the central core tighter and tighter. The rest of the star expands many times, turning it into a red giant. This is a very large star with a relatively low surface temperature. The outer layers drift off into space, leaving a small, densely packed white dwarf, which slowly cools and becomes the size of a small planet.

Larger stars with a mass more than 10 times greater than the sun's have much shorter lives because they burn hydrogen much faster. Many of these stars form an iron core, which explodes into a supernova. The mass expelled from a supernova is far more tightly packed than even a white dwarf. When the diameter of that remaining mass shrinks to 10 to 20 miles (16.1–32.2 km), the object becomes an extremely hot neutron star.

Even larger stars undergo a similar process, but their cores are ultimately pressed even tighter. The neutrons at the center, densely packed though they are, can't resist the inward push of gravity, and the star collapses completely. For almost 200 years, no one was certain what to call this

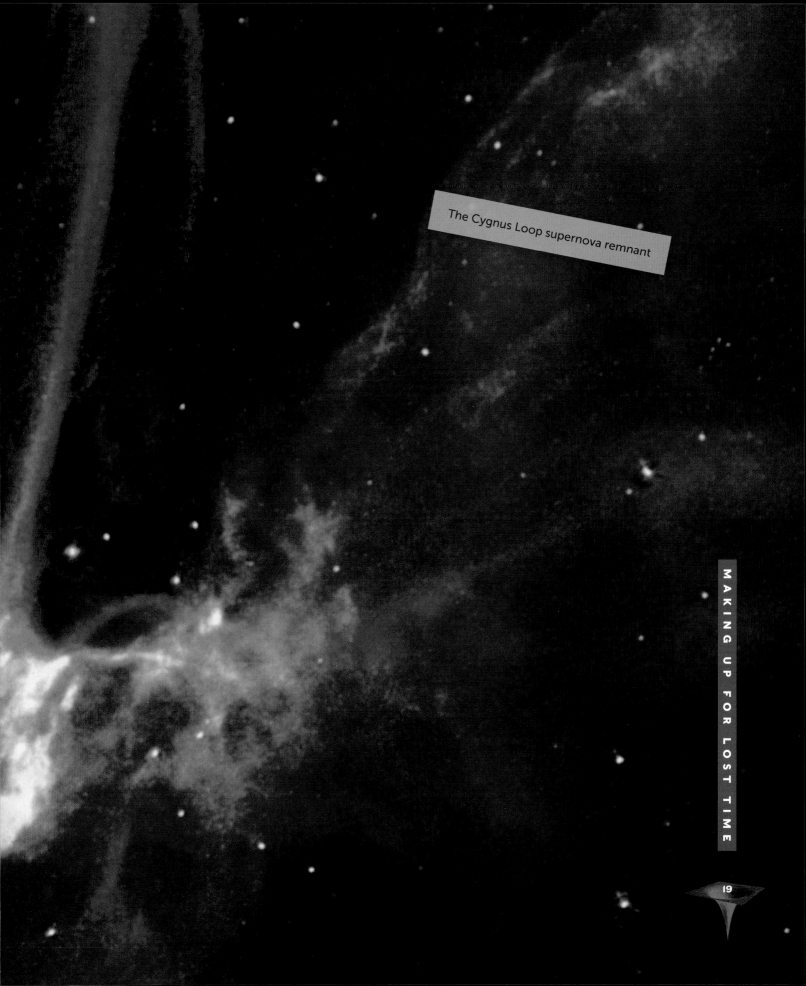

The Cygnus Loop supernova remnant

19

An artist's idea of what Cygnus X-1 looks like

Scheduled for launch in 2021, the International X-ray Observatory (IXO) will give scientists studying black holes a powerful new research tool. The IXO is being developed jointly by the National Aeronautics and Space Administration (NASA), the European Space Agency (ESA), and the Japan Aerospace Exploration Agency (JAXA). The IXO will perform complicated experiments to provide astrophysicists with invaluable information about the origins and evolution of matter and energy. One of the major goals is to learn more about supermassive black holes (SMBH), which should aid in studying the formation and development of **galaxies**. X-rays are useful for studying black holes and other astronomical phenomena because they can penetrate solid objects, something no other form of electromagnetic energy can do. They can also easily pass through interstellar gas and dust, which block light rays (thereby putting severe limitations on optical telescopes) and other forms of electromagnetic energy. However, X-rays cannot pierce Earth's atmosphere, so the IXO must be launched into outer space. From its orbit around Earth, it will be able to beam its rays without interruption or interference into the deepest parts of the universe. Scientists believe the IXO will function effectively for at least 5 years and perhaps as many as 10.

third phenomenon. Terms such as "frozen stars" and "collapsars" were often used, but there wasn't anything that everyone could agree on until 1967 when Wheeler came up with "black hole." As he explains in his book *A Journey into Gravity and Spacetime*, the change "was terminologically trivial but psychologically powerful. After the name was introduced, more and more astronomers and astrophysicists came to appreciate that black holes might not be a figment of the imagination but astronomical objects worth spending time and money to seek."

Such seeking soon paid off. In 1971, astronomers discovered X-rays being produced by a **binary star** in the constellation Cygnus (the Swan), which is about 6,000 **light years** from Earth. They named this source Cygnus X-1. A huge star named HDE 226 868, perhaps 30 times the size of the sun, is nearby. It seems likely that, at one point, these stars made up a two-star system. Now they are linked by a long trail of gas that Cygnus X-1 rips from its companion as it orbits. This gas speeds up and gets hotter the closer it gets to the black hole, eventually becoming hot enough to generate X-rays

Spain's Great Canary Telescope detects visible and infrared light

before being sucked into the black hole.

The discovery of the activity of Cygnus X-1 illustrates one way that astronomers are able to detect black holes, since they cannot see them directly. Because X-rays are invisible to the naked eye, certain telescopes known as X-ray telescopes are designed to detect X-ray emissions. X-rays may not guarantee the presence of a black hole, but they provide strong evidence that one may exist.

y the 1990s, astronomers had figured out that another way of detecting a black hole is by looking at the way that surrounding stars behave. If a black hole is nearby, it can cause a star to speed up as it orbits the black hole. The more massive the black hole, the faster the star moves in its orbit. This method of deduction led to the discovery that V404 Cygnus, a star close to Cygnus X-1, has a companion black hole much larger than the star itself.

Around that same time, astronomers began suspecting that black holes of almost unimaginable size existed at the center of many—if not nearly all—galaxies. These became known as supermassive black holes (SMBH), and, according to some estimates, they might contain the mass of hundreds of millions of suns. In particular, research centered on Sagittarius A*, which is located between the constellations of Sagittarius and Scorpius about 27,000 light years away from Earth at the heart of the Milky Way.

agittarius A* was the subject of a painstaking 16-year study that concluded in 2008. A team of astronomers from Germany's Max-Planck-Institute for **Extraterrestrial** Physics used telescopes capable of detecting **infrared** light to penetrate the thick cosmic dust that lies between Earth and the galaxy's center. With a degree of accuracy equivalent to spotting a quarter from more than 6,000 miles (10,000 km) away, the astronomers followed the paths of 28 stars to determine the forces that were acting on them. In the process, they learned a great deal about the formation and operation of black holes—and possibly confirmed their very existence. "Undoubtedly the most spectacular aspect of our long-term study is that it has delivered what is now considered to be the best **empirical evidence** that supermassive black holes do really exist," said astrophysicist and team leader Reinhard Genzel.

More exciting news about black holes was announced in 2010. Astronomers from the National Aeronautics and Space Administration (NASA) said they had witnessed the birth of a black hole—relatively speaking, that is. Because it is 50 million light years away, the supernova explosion that led to the black hole actually happened long ago, but to astronomers, that hardly matters. "We've never known before the exact birthday of a black hole, and now we can watch as it grows into a child and teenager," explained

White dwarf stars in the Milky Way

The Chandra X-ray Observatory

An SMBH (central black dot) in early stages

In 1935, a young Indian scientist named Subrahmanyan Chandrasekhar (1910–95) presented a groundbreaking idea to a meeting of the prestigious Royal Astronomical Society in London, England. He proved mathematically that only stars 1.44 times the mass of the sun or less could become white dwarfs. "For a star of small mass the natural white dwarf stage is an initial step towards complete extinction," he explained.

"A star of large mass cannot pass into the white dwarf stage, and one is left speculating on other possibilities." Moments later, Sir Arthur Eddington (1882–1944)—a leading scientific figure of that era and a man whom Chandrasekhar had regarded as a friend—ridiculed him, saying, "I think there should be a law of Nature to prevent a star from behaving in this absurd way!" Chandrasekhar was depressed by this response and didn't pursue

those "other possibilities," which eventually resulted in the discovery of black holes. He moved on to other areas of research related to massive stars, yet he had the last laugh. He was awarded the 1983 Nobel Prize in Physics, an honor Eddington never attained. Additionally, the Chandra X-ray Observatory—named in his honor—was launched into space in 1999 and has since made many valuable discoveries about stars and black holes.

NASA astrophysicist Kimberly Weaver. "Learning about black holes has been like solving a puzzle, and this will help us get closer to a full understanding."

Black holes are fascinating enough as they are, yet there's one more aspect that makes them almost irresistible to many people: wormholes. Wormholes are the theoretical connections that may exist between two black holes laid end to end. Because they would act as bridges between space and time, some scientists believe that wormholes might make time travel possible and reveal new dimensions, universes, or time periods. While time travel sounds like something ripped from the pages of a **science fiction** novel, some noted researchers in the study of black holes have given the concept serious consideration.

English physicist Isaac Newton

SHEDDING LIGHT ON BLACK HOLES

The process of identifying and understanding black holes began with English physicist Isaac Newton (1643–1727). Sitting in his orchard one day in 1666, he watched an apple fall from a tree. That observation led him to realize that everything with mass exerts a gravitational pull on all other masses. The greater the mass of a particular object, the stronger its gravitational pull. Therefore, Earth pulled the apple downward rather than the other way around. Newton was the first person to realize that this force extended to the farthest reaches of the universe.

Newton then employed complicated mathematical formulas to show that the strength of gravity for a particular body varies according to both its mass and the distance between the center of that body and its perimeter, or edge. It follows that, if an object can be compressed, or flattened, by pressure and made very tiny without sacrificing any of its mass, it will achieve an incredibly strong gravitational pull.

English clergyman and **natural philosopher** John Michell (1724–93) may have begun the search for black holes during the 1780s. Being familiar with Newton's findings, he knew that if a cannonball or some other object was propelled upward, gravity would slow its ascent, and it would crash back down to Earth. If it could attain escape velocity—a concept well understood in that era—it would continue upward and eventually release itself from the pull of gravity.

Michell imagined a star with the same **density** of the sun but a **radius** 500 times larger. He theorized that this star's escape velocity would be so great that light could never leave it. In a letter to English scientist Henry Cavendish in 1783, Michell wrote, "Let us now suppose the **particles** of light to be attracted in the same manner as all other bodies with which we are acquainted.... All light emitted from such a body would be made to return towards it, by its own proper gravity." Michell realized that, if he was correct, we could never see such "dark stars" because they would not give off any light.

Michell had the right idea but the wrong reasoning. He thought a star had to be huge for its gravity to swallow up light. No one has ever discovered a star that immense, and in all likelihood it would be a physical impossibility. Instead, the key to the mystery lay in the incredible amount of shrinkage of mass that had to occur to create a black hole. Michell also thought some double-star systems would contain a dark star and that astronomers should search for cases in which a single star was visible. His idea for calculating the number of such "invisible" stars anticipated the work of modern astronomers.

In 1796, French mathematician and astronomer Pierre Laplace (1749–1827) developed a theory almost identical to Michell's, even though he had apparently never heard of the Englishman. Laplace called black holes "hidden bodies" instead. But like Michell, he accepted Newton's theory that light was formed of particles. However, an 1801 experiment by English physicist Thomas Young (1773–1829) demonstrated that light was composed of waves, rather than particles. Since the era's prevailing belief was that gravity had no effect on waves, any interest in dark stars or hidden bodies quickly disappeared.

After Einstein's general theory of relativity was published in 1915, German physicist Karl Schwarzschild (1873–1916) applied the complicated equations Einstein had used in developing the general theory to arrive at some further startling results. Schwarzschild demonstrated mathematically that, as a star collapsed, at some point it would curve space and time so much that nothing could ever escape. This point eventually became known as the Schwarzschild radius, the distance from the event horizon to the singularity. Schwarzschild also showed that any object could in theory become a black hole—including Earth, if it somehow became compressed into a ball half an inch (1 cm) across. Despite Schwarzschild's carefully worked-out proofs, many scientists chose to believe that black holes didn't exist. Einstein was especially firm in his denial. In 1939, he published a paper based on his gravitational theories entitled "On a Stationary System with Spherical Symmetry Consisting of Many Gravitating Masses." At the heart of this

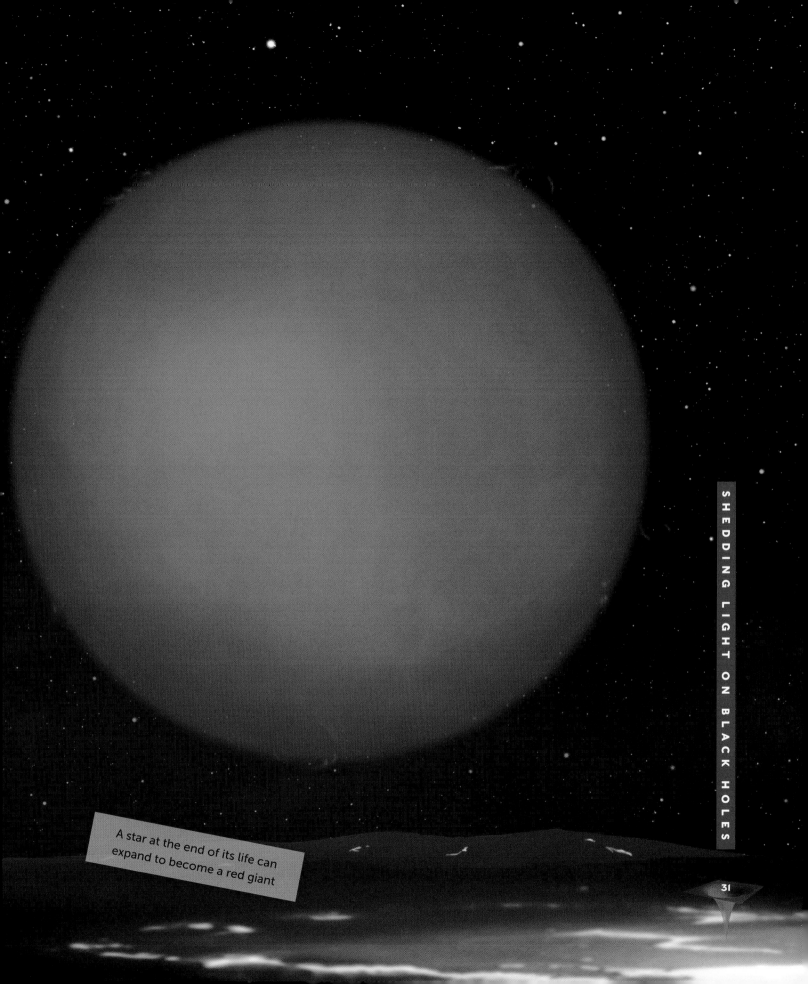

A star at the end of its life can expand to become a red giant

paper was the simple message that there were no such things as black holes.

A few months later, at the University of California, Berkeley, American physicist J. Robert Oppenheimer (1904–67) and his student Hartland Snyder (1913–62) used Einstein's equations to conclude the opposite. According to their calculations, a massive star would continue to shrink as it used up its hydrogen fuel. Eventually it would **implode** until it was smaller than its Schwarzschild radius, pulling space and time around it as it disappeared from view.

Events then intervened that would halt further discoveries about black holes for decades. World War II broke out that same year, and Oppenheimer and many other scientists of the day became consumed with the application of atomic power in weapons. Wheeler's introduction of the term "black holes" in 1967 finally returned attention to the phenomenon. Wheeler also said, "black holes have no hair." What he meant by that curious statement is that we often use hair as a way of telling two otherwise identical people apart. But the force of gravity in a black hole "shaves off"

Albert Einstein and J. Robert Oppenheimer

the distinguishing properties of objects, such as their shape and chemical composition. It leaves only the object's mass, its speed of spinning, and its electrical charge.

Wheeler also used an **analogy** to help explain how astronomers could tell that black holes belonged to two-star systems, as Michell had theorized. In a dimly lit ballroom, women in white dresses are partnered with men in black tuxedos. Although an observer cannot see the men, watching the women spin and whirl around something indicates that the men are there. Black holes are thus like the men in black tuxedos, while the detectable objects around them are like the women in white dresses.

In 1974, noted British physicist and author Stephen Hawking (1942–) put forward a bold theory: black holes would eventually evaporate and perhaps even explode. According to Hawking, black holes aren't completely black, or without light or energy. That's because the energy of a black hole continually generates particles. These particles have corresponding antiparticles, which are their exact opposite and therefore cancel each other out. Generally, particles and antiparticles in black holes collide in a fraction of a second, thereby destroying each other. But near the event horizon, one of the pair might be sucked downward, while the other escapes. For example, an **electron** could radiate outward as heat energy, while a positron (its opposite that carries a positive charge) would fall back inward. Since the escaping particle contains energy, and—as Einstein demonstrated in his famous equation $E=mc^2$ (energy equals mass times the speed of light squared, or multiplied by itself)—energy is the same as mass, the black hole loses a tiny bit of mass every time a particle escapes.

This process of losing mass while emitting heat energy is known as Hawking radiation. Over time—perhaps billions of years—the black hole shrinks, and this shrinkage accelerates as the hole grows continuously smaller. Then it explodes with the strength of hundreds of millions of hydrogen bombs. Thus far, no exploding black holes have been identified, so Hawking radiation remains in the realm of theory for now.

Stephen Hawking, pictured in 2008

SHEDDING LIGHT ON BLACK HOLES

A magnet core of one of the particle detectors on the Large Hadron Collider

BLACK HOLES IN THE FUTURE

Because black holes are a comparatively recent development, a great deal of information remains to be discovered, and many theories require proof. One example is another of Hawking's theories that argues for the existence of mini black holes, which have the mass of a mountain packed into the size of an atom's nucleus. These mini black holes are thought to have formed just after the **Big Bang** and may be on the verge of exploding. Such an explosion would release gamma rays, and if these rays could be observed in some way, it would provide a small-scale glimpse into the Big Bang and therefore the origins of the universe. While astronomers have detected gamma rays from many objects in space, they can't specifically identify any of these as coming from mini black holes. Some scientists believe creating a mini black hole in a laboratory setting would be the best way of studying the phenomenon's potential.

To accomplish this, scientists would use **colliders**, such as the Large Hadron Collider belonging to the European Organization for Nuclear Research (CERN), to accelerate **subatomic** particles to nearly the speed of light and then smash them into each other. The collision would generate a momentary burst of energy and extremely high temperatures, mimicking the conditions under which mini black holes are formed. If this process were successful, colliders could act as black hole "factories," producing one tiny black hole after another in rapid succession.

Most black hole research originates in outer space, though, and it's a rare month that doesn't include the announcement of yet another discovery. Early in 2011, for example, a team of astronomers from the California Institute of Technology (Caltech), the University of Illinois at Urbana-Champaign, and the University of Hawaii discovered 16 pairs of SMBH in merging galaxies. They were at least 100 times closer than any previously observed. According to Caltech staff member Lin Yan, "Our results add to the growing understanding of how galaxies and their central black holes evolve."

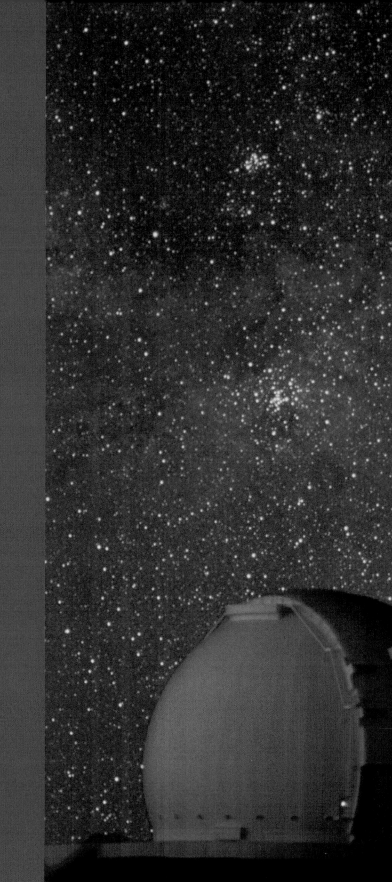

Another area of continuing research involves quasars, formerly known as quasi-stellar radio sources. First discovered in 1963, quasars didn't fit into the established pattern of stars that existed at the time. All that was known was that they looked extremely bright, extremely small, and extremely far away. Further research revealed that quasars are the remnants of distant and highly active galaxies and that they contain massive black holes. Astronomer Alan Stockton of the University of Hawaii, Honolulu, assisted by graduate student Hai Fu, is currently seeking the origins of the massive amounts of gas that quasars eject. Using the Gemini telescopes (one in Hawaii, the other in Chile), Stockton and Fu believe that at least some of this gas could come from material in other, more distant galaxies.

Much of the research on quasars and black holes is of interest primarily to astronomers and physicists. The

Hawaii's clear skies make it a perfect location for telescopes

An artist's vision of a wormhole

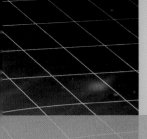

Making *Contact* through Wormholes

The central character of Carl Sagan's 1985 science fiction novel *Contact* is Eleanor "Ellie" Arroway. She directs Project Argus, which uses a series of **radio telescopes** to search for extraterrestrial intelligence. She receives a message from aliens and builds a machine to meet with them. In an early version of the book, Sagan had Ellie travel through a black hole to make contact. He asked black hole researcher Kip Thorne if this was feasible. Thorne explained that anyone who tried to journey through a black hole would be destroyed and suggested that Sagan use wormholes for Ellie's journey instead. He provided Sagan with some ideas about what a wormhole might look like. Sagan took Thorne's advice, and the book became a best seller. Sagan was perhaps the best-known scientist of his era, with several popular nonfiction titles and many television appearances to his credit, so he received a $2-million **advance** from his publisher. At the time, it was the largest advance ever given for an unwritten book. *Locus* magazine, a science fiction and fantasy publication, named *Contact* the best first novel of 1985. In 1997, the book was made into a film of the same name, starring Jodie Foster and Matthew McConaughey.

possibility of time travel is a notable exception, as it crosses the boundaries of science and popular culture. Books and movies that deal with moving back and forth through time have been popular for many years, even before the discovery of black holes made it theoretically possible. Many versions of time travel rest on the concept of wormholes, the passages between two black holes.

The science underpinning the possibility of time travel began to emerge in 1935, when Einstein and American-Israeli physicist Nathan Rosen created the first model of what a wormhole might look like. Even though Einstein had long disclaimed the possibility of black holes, he and Rosen set up something similar by using mathematical calculations that suggested that a black hole's center could match up with the center of an identical black hole in another universe. Rather than being crushed in a black hole, therefore, cosmic adventurers could use this passage to travel safely. This solution, first known as the Einstein-Rosen Bridge, was later popularized by the name "wormhole." Calculations by Wheeler showed that such a concept would be fundamentally flawed, though. Nothing, not even a ray of light, would be able to make it through a wormhole because the force of gravity would cause the wormhole to collapse almost instantaneously.

In 1988, inspired by his friend Carl Sagan's novel *Contact*, Caltech theoretical physicist Kip Thorne suggested a way to stabilize wormholes. If some kind of antigravity substance with negative energy could push back the walls of the wormhole against the force of gravity, then the wormhole would remain open. Thorne's position also depended on the theory that Earth is on a gently curving, two-dimensional plane in hyperspace (a space of more than three dimensions—in Thorne's case, six). For example, while the bright star Vega is more than 26 light years away in normal space, in hyperspace it could be connected via a 0.6-mile (1 km) wormhole to Earth. It would be similar to the effect of doubling a rug over on itself. When the rug is flat, two points are far away from each other. When the rug is folded, the two points become much closer.

ven more recently, Israeli-born physicist Lior Burko has taken a different approach to the concept of traveling through a black hole. Disagreeing with the traditional view that the singularity of a black hole rips everything to shreds, Burko seeks evidence for **hybrid** singularities, with strong areas (where everything is destroyed) and weak ones (where gravity's pull is slightly reduced). If a spacecraft were traveling through the universe toward the black hole, according to Burko, a hybrid singularity "would allow the captain to navigate toward the sector where the singularity is weak. Experiencing only finite (and even small) effects (of stretching and squeezing), the spaceship could arrive at the singularity unharmed. While that still does not guarantee a peaceful traversing of the singularity, it keeps the possibility of doing so open. If that traversing becomes possible, it could open a 'tunnel' to another universe."

Burko has further explained that stellar black holes, or black holes resulting from

Actress Jodie Foster as Ellie Arroway in Contact

Breaking New Movie Ground

Released in 1979, the Disney movie *The Black Hole* begins with the spaceship USS *Palomino* returning to Earth in the year 2130 after an 18-month mission to search for extraterrestrial life. The *Palomino* finds the USS *Cygnus*, which disappeared 20 years earlier, hovering near a black hole. An antigravity force field on the *Cygnus* keeps it from being sucked into the black hole. The *Palomino* docks with the *Cygnus*, whose commander, Dr. Hans Reinhardt, behaves mysteriously. The spacecraft appears to be run by robots, but the *Palomino* crew soon learns that Reinhardt and a robot named Maximilian have "reprogrammed" the *Cygnus* crew members to control a mutiny after Reinhardt disobeyed an order to return to Earth. Eventually, Reinhardt says he wants to take the *Cygnus* into the black hole. The *Palomino* crew opposes him, and that leads to a final conflict between the two crews. The film's opening credits included the longest computer-generated imagery scene in a movie up to that time. *The Black Hole* was nominated for two Academy Awards—in visual effects and cinematography—though it didn't win either one. It was also the first Disney film to show humans dying. Late in 2009, Disney announced plans to film a new version of *The Black Hole*.

a single star, aren't good candidates for having hybrid singularities. He prefers the conditions at the SMBH of Sagittarius A*, where the gravitational forces may not be as strong in some areas as they are in others. Unfortunately, getting there would be a problem, since it's so far away. It would require not only a super-fast spaceship but also the likelihood of producing several generations of people during the long voyage.

Scientists will continue to study black holes and SMBH, seeking clues as to their origins in hopes of someday shedding light on the origins (and perhaps the eventual fate) of the universe. Because the nature of black holes remains so mysterious, the possibilities of what future study may reveal are boundless. Some people, for example, think that black holes could become future sources of energy, though it would be difficult to harness such energy across the vast reaches of space. One solution to the distance problem would be to construct a settlement near a black hole but far enough away to ensure that it didn't approach the event horizon. Mini black holes may be a more feasible future source of energy, especially if they can be created in Earth-bound laboratories.

Whether they may one day be used for energy or as a means of providing access to other universes, black holes are among the most fascinating subjects of study in the entire universe. They excite the imaginations of scientists and non-scientists in ways that few other stellar subjects can approach. Future discoveries will only add to their allure.

ENDNOTES

advance — money paid to an author before publication of a book in anticipation that the book will sell enough copies to at least cover the amount of the advance

analogy — a comparison between two entities to show similarities or to explain their structure

astrophysicist — a person who studies the branch of astronomy that deals with the physical nature of the universe

atom — the smallest part of an element with the chemical properties of that element

Big Bang — a theory that the universe was in a highly compressed state about 13.7 billion years ago and then exploded with great force, releasing huge amounts of matter that eventually formed stars and planets

binary star — a stellar system in which two stars revolve around a common center and may appear as a single object

buffoonery — acting like a clown or an idiot

colliders — devices that accelerate subatomic particles to nearly the speed of light and are linear or circular in shape

density — the mass per unit volume measured in a substance

electromagnetic spectrum — the range of wavelengths produced by electrical and magnetic currents in space that carry energy

electron — a tiny, negatively charged particle that orbits the nucleus, or center, of an atom

empirical evidence — proof based on experience or observation

extraterrestrial — originating or occurring outside Earth

galaxies — systems of stars held together by mutual gravitational attraction and separated from similar systems by vast regions of space

gamma rays — the shortest waves on the electromagnetic spectrum; they can be generated by radioactive materials and nuclear explosions

hybrid — something made by combining two or more different elements

implode — to collapse inward

infinitesimal — an amount or quantity too small to be measured or calculated

infrared — a type of light that cannot be seen by humans; its wavelength is longer than visible light's

light years — the distance light travels in a year, which is nearly 6 trillion miles (9.7 trillion km)

natural philosopher — a person who studies the nature and functioning of the universe

nuclear fusion — a process in which four hydrogen atoms fuse, or combine, under intense temperatures and pressure to form one helium atom and give off heat and light

orbit — the curved path that a celestial object takes around a larger celestial object

particles — the smallest pieces or traces of something

physicist — a person who studies matter and motion through space and time in an effort to discover the physical laws of the universe

radio telescopes — a group of radio antennas designed to detect and measure radio waves from celestial sources

radio waves — the longest waves on the electromagnetic spectrum; they can be used for communicating in radio, television, and cell phones

radius — the distance from the center of a circle or sphere to the perimeter, or edge

science fiction — a type of fiction writing in which scientific principles or discoveries play an important role

subatomic — occurring in or smaller than an atom

supernova — an exploding giant star; remnants are blasted out into space and become the basis for new stars

WEB SITES

Ask an Astrophysicist: Black Holes
http://imagine.gsfc.nasa.gov/docs/ask_astro/black_holes.html
Get all your black hole questions answered here, and find new resources for further research.

CERN LHC: Facts and Figures
http://public.web.cern.ch/public/en/lhc/Facts-en.html
Fill your brain with facts about the Large Hadron Collider, and download a brochure for more information.

SELECTED BIBLIOGRAPHY

Begelman, Mitchell, and Martin Rees. *Gravity's Fatal Attraction: Black Holes in the Universe*. New York: Scientific American Library, 1996.

Couper, Heather, and Nigel Henbest. *The History of Astronomy*. Buffalo, N.Y.: Firefly Books, 2007.

Hawking, Stephen, and Leonard Mlodinow. *A Briefer History of Time*. New York: Bantam Books, 2005.

Miller, Arthur. *Empire of the Stars: Obsession, Friendship and Betrayal in the Quest for Black Holes*. New York: Houghton Mifflin, 2005.

Pickover, Clifford A. *Black Holes: A Traveler's Guide*. New York: John Wiley & Sons, 1996.

Thorne, Kip S. *Black Holes and Time Warps: Einstein's Outrageous Legacy*. New York: W. W. Norton, 1994.

Tyson, Neil DeGrasse. *Death by Black Hole and Other Cosmic Quandaries*. New York: W. W. Norton, 2007.

Wheeler, John. *A Journey into Gravity and Spacetime*. New York: Scientific American Library, 1990.

INDEX